HIV isn't POETIC

POEMS ON A LIFE WITH hiV

BY JONATHAN W. THURSTON-TORRES

FENRIS
™

HIV isn't poetic

Copyright © 2023 by Jonathan W. Thurston-Torres

Published by Fenris Publishing
Flagstaff, Arizona
https://www.fenrispublishing.com

ISBN 978-1-62475-171-4
Printed in the United States, United Kingdom, or Australia
First trade paperback edition: May 2023

Cover art by Taurin Fox
Edited by David M. Sula

Contents

The Cute Guy Who Was Friends With My Boyfriend

We had talked for a couple of weeks,
Adam in Memphis and me in Murfreesboro,
when he texted me the question out of the blue:

so are you hiv poz too?

My heart plummeted
nine times the space of day and night
and broke somewhere along
the fault.

I was dogsitting for a friend,
and the world was electrons in high energy—
buzzing—
I felt danger.

And the dogs stayed asleep by the couch.

I learned things over the next thirty-six hours:
My boyfriend had cheated on me.
My boyfriend was living with the guy.
As far as this other guy knew, I didn't exist.
The guy had HIV.
My boyfriend had HIV,
and he knew about it for years.
I had/ve HIV.

My heart tumbled down the fault,
but whose fault was it?

HIV isn't poetic

I got the call to the doctor's office
January 7, 2015
sat in the waiting room
waiting

when I got called back, I
sat in another room
in a chair
fearing
expecting
the worst

a nurse came in

she didn't close the door
she didn't sit down
she didn't look at me
just down

at her clipboard

"Well, Mr. Thurston, your tests came back positive for HIV. Is
there anything else we can help you with today?"

nothing poetic about that, is there

"Um, no thanks," was all I said

a part of me is still dead in that chair
still hopeful that all this is a dream

the rest of me is a zombie
walking dead

Phone Call in the Night

My first night back home,
I wanted to kill myself.

I wanted to kill myself
so
bad.

Sitting in my underwear
on bathroom tile,
my hands wrenching my hair,
my face twisted in pain.

I called Dustin.

I have HIV. My ex lied to me.

He didn't know what to do,
any more than I did.

but that silence was

everything.

Guilty

I remember calling the Murfreesboro Police Department
one day to see if they could stop him from doing this again,

to someone else, someone besides me,
so I told them what happened.

And they said sorry, sorry because he
lived in Memphis and was therefore outside

their jurisdiction. So I tried the Memphis police,
and they said the same since I was outside theirs.

But they didn't hang up before they let me know
that the fault was mine.

"You really should have known this was a possibility if you were
going to have gay sex."

Just saying

A few nights a week, I would cook.
Mostly for myself.
Usually for myself.
But often, I'd make extra
for the roommates.
And the apartment was welcome
to have some of whatever I made.

Pasta marinara.
Curry.
Soups and stews.
Whatever.
Donovan ate it.
Nathan ate it.
Alicia ate it.

Then, I got HIV.

Suddenly, Alicia started washing dishes with disposable gloves on.
Suddenly, she stopped eating my food.
"Did I make something bad? Do you not like my cooking
anymore?"

"No. I just don't want to get HIV from eating food you cook.
And, if I were you, I wouldn't be having sex with anyone any-
more. Just saying."

Those words still ring in my ears and in my heart,
and every time I cook for someone—
whether it's friends or family or even students or my professors—
I always wonder if, when they look down at the plate,
if they're wondering if they'll get HIV.

There's too much salt in my tears
for me to be able to swallow
this meal.

"Just saying."

Things You Might Say to a Friend

Whenever I catch a cold,
There are things that I am told:
Poor thing. Get some rest.
Chicken soup is prob'ly best.

Whenever I get strep,
I get a list, step by step:
Drink fluids. Get lots of sleep.
And don't you dare make a peep.

And when someone gets cancer,
What do you say in answer?
I'm so, so sorry. What stage?
Maybe it just came with age.

Diabetes is another common thing,
What advice can you bring?
Try exercise. Try diets.
You won't know 'til you try it.

And HIV?
What do you say
to someone with that?

I'll tell you what I've heard: You shouldn't have kept your legs
open. You shouldn't have been
gay. You shouldn't have trusted him when he said he didn't have
it. You shouldn't worry because it's not as bad as it used to be.
You should kill yourself. Why don't you kill yourself? Why are
you here, infecting all those around you, you're the reason peo-
ple don't like gays. Kill yourself.

RIP

It's funny how HIV looks just like RIP when chatting on an app, typing
the letters because the law says you have to, typing
what for some has been a death warrant, typing
your medical record for someone else, typing
when HIV isn't their type.

Look up how Ceceila Bolden was killed by her husband, bleeding
just like Todd Heywood when he was beat up, bleeding
from the hands of some homophobic killers, bleeding
while they said he deserved to die, still bleeding,
because of what was in his blood.

And after my online confession, you'll stop responding, swiping
along the keyboard without a single worry or care, swiping
left so that you don't have to see me again, swiping
me off-screen into the digital abyss, swiping
my identity into a digital grave, swiping
some dirt off the edge, swiping
me six feet under,
my voice
swiped.

And yet, after that confession, I still hope beyond reason, praying
that blocking me is the worst that they'll do, praying
that they won't lie and ask my address, praying
they don't make me their prey.

It's funny how HIV looks just like RIP.

The Grindr Graveyard

it's quiet in the cemetery
of souls lost because
of disclosure of their
diagnosis. disclosing
gets them killed.
they're beaten.
they're imprisoned.
they're murdered.
every fucking time
i tell someone
on Grindr,
i wonder:

will i be next?

I Asked for It

1

My profile said it all: "23yo kinky college student looking for love, hiv-undetectable." NashvilPred236 and I chatted for a month. And it felt great. Someone who didn't judge me for a medical chart and didn't care that I had this curse I never asked for and didn't ask me to explain everything to him. And it felt great to be looked at like I wasn't a walking-dead virus. He saw me for my love of books and my love of Disney and my love of Japanese food. So he met me there at a little hole-in-the-wall sushi place off Gallatin Pike. We talked, and he was even more magical in person and I said wow I'm so glad to meet someone who doesn't judge me for my HIV status or anything like that and oh my Satan it's so refreshing to be treated like a—Huh? Uh, yeah, I have HIV. It's on my profile...He pulls out the phone and puts on the app and suddenly my head is spinning in the silence and when he doesn't look up and just lays twenties on the table just as the food comes out and leaves, I start to cry. When I try the sushi for two, I'm not sure if I taste soy sauce or tears. I cried on the way home.

2

After sex one time the guy asked how I got pozzed who pozzed me how it happened how it happened to the detail and he wanted to know if my partner had lied about his status and he wanted to know if I had wanted it and he wanted to know why I didn't wear protection and he wanted me to know that he wished he could have been the one to poz me. — He didn't know that I want to be loved despite my HIV not because of it. He wouldn't let me leave until I promised to call him back. I blocked his number when I got to my car. And cried.

3

I met a guy who scared me once. We talked limits first and I came over and everything was great. He tied me up and used me and made me feel good and bad and rough and raw and full despite my emptiness. And then he whispered in my ear and told me that he actually had no plans of letting me leave. This wasn't the plan. He kept going. He told me he wanted to make me drop out of school and stay there with me as his permanent house slave, always caged, used by his friends when they came over and he told me I was wasting my "purpose" with school when I should really be there to serve him and I just kept trying to look through the haze for a weapon I could use but when he came, his facade broke, and he was just a sweetheart. But we hadn't talked about that happening up front. And I was still scared. When I walked out the door, I was still scared. I haven't stopped being scared. Oh my Satan I never stopped.

4

I talk to adamsman100 for a good month sharing kinks and interests so when a night opens up and I'm horny for it I message him and we talk about the essentials—what all we planned to get into that night, my limits, my safe words and signs—and I text a friend my address and I head over. Once I'm there, he cuffs my thumbs together—I remember how tight they were and how they cut into my skin—and he pushes me to the ground and he and his friend fuck me and they fuck me too rough and I start using my safe words this wasn't what we talked about this wasn't the plan and his labrador was in the room with us and he says, if you don't shut up, I'll make my dog rape you too. So I lie there. And take it. And I know, no Tennessee judge would see my messages about kink from the past month and say I hadn't asked for it. Not in Tennessee. I take it and cry when I get home. I rub my thumbs.

5

March 2021 I talk to Ready? on Grindr for a day and we meet up in the driveway of my house and I slide into the passenger's seat and he fucks my throat till he cums then leaves. Then he texts me again wanting a second round so I go back out and he fucks me in the back seat. Two weeks later I'm at a friend's house when he messages me: Hey. I say Hey, and we talk about hooking up again and this time, the only time, he asks if I am "clean" and I say that of course I am and I don't have anything except I am HIV undetectable which is basically clean according to the CDC and—DAMN WTF MAN ARE YOU SERIOUS—Yeah, but you're seriously fine. I can't spread it because I'm on medicati—FUCKK FOR REAL???—Yeah, but really, I don't mind sending you the CDC link for—NO DUDE DID YOU SERIOUSLY GIVE ME AIDS—No—WHY DIDN'T YOU TELL ME—It was on my Grindr profile. I sigh, and explain, and maybe fail or maybe succeed, and after a half an hour of this conversation, and he says—Oh okay, well I wanna see you again. Are you home right now?—...What?—Right now, are you home? Where are you?—I don't answer. I stay silent. And I drive home, 3am, and hope there's not someone waiting in my driveway to kill me. Hope I don't come home to see my house on fire. And whether it was fire or a gunshot, had I asked for it? I rub my thumbs on the way home.

I'll Pray for You

I've heard a lot of I'll pray for you.

I don't want a divine power to fix me.
I don't want an invisible man to show me the way.
I don't want a 2,000-year-old book to beat me
       into submission.
I don't want your thoughts and prayers.

My god tells me I'm on my own.
He tells me to suck it up.
He tells me to suck his dick.
On all fours, I kneel and spread my legs.
I grasp his horns and don't beg for anything—
       not forgiveness or compassion or help—
except for him to take me harder
and breed me full of his little goat-man seed.

I don't want promises of a cloudy heaven
full of angelic choirs and freedom from my bodily prison.

I want a gay club without closing hours
where the bar makes vanilla lattes with extra espresso
and the temperature is hot and the men are even hotter
and the fist-fucking in slings is hot and steamy and just right
and my god checks in with me and asks if I am all right
and if I say "no," he doesn't treat me like I'm broken.

Instead, he offers me a hand—or a hoof—
and asks if I want to dance.
Because sometimes, sometimes,
being numb is better than being fixed.

       Abandon all hope, ye who enter here.

Who needs hope when I have a home?

"you're diseased and you want all that? well arent you a picky little bitch?" —some guy on Grindr

Humble Pie

People act so surprised when I say I speak against stigmatizing HIV. People say I should cease having standards and take any guy, anyone who doesn't mind getting HIV. Hell, I heard it on a hookup app once. Maybe twice. Maybe more. And I still hear it. Lower your standards. But I'm sick of getting stood up in darkened driveways and hearing dates talk about how their irritable bowel syndrome is like my immune system and being told I'm not good enough. So no, I won't sit down and take what I can get. No. Every sick cell in my body is still sexy.

unclean

"open relationship" he said

i felt relieved
i had missed sex
i had missed embraces
and touches
and kisses
and cum

"just as long as you communicate" he said

me?
i couldn't agree more
i wanted to tell him
stories
of love and lust
and adventures
and action
but instead
i promised
to tell him where i'd go
and when i'd go
and when to expect me back
and i knew
he'd keep me safe
he'd check in on me
he'd call the police
if i went missing
or died

weeks passed
we were doing good

"hey babe, is it okay if i go out on a hookup tonight?" i said

i had needs
and a guy on grindr
did too

"sure, that's fine. just let me know where and when you're on
your way back" he said

i did all we had said
told him the place
told him when
even told him who the guy was
told him when i'd be back
and it was a good time
i had a good time

"on my way home" i texted

i missed him
i wanted comfort
i wanted him to
tell me
we were good
and we'd be together
a while yet

"i'm home" i said

i reached out to hug him
he pulled away

he pulled
so far
away

"i don't want to touch you" he said

like a hammer
slamming a nail

i froze
my heart froze

"you're unclean" he said.

Streets and Sheets

Part of the struggle of being a hypersexual grad student
is just about everything.

Grindr is made up of chests and pants and blanks
And "discrete only" and "anon," which is to say blanks.
When I have sex, I rarely see the guy's face.
I sent him my face online.
He sent me his dick.
He could be a student or a colleague or faculty,
And I'd never know.
But he would.

Sex clubs are full of naked bodies.
Dark spaces   gloryholes
        and without my glasses faces dissolve.
    Just
                        blurs.

In a place where 90% of communication is nonverbal,
What do I say? "Sorry, can I see your ID to make sure you don't
go to my school? I go to MSU. If you do, too, we can't fuck."
End scene.

On my Twitter, I post underwear selfies. Sometimes less.
Does that mean I can't be professional?
Does that mean I can't talk about Foucault
or Derrida
or discourse?

Why must a life of sexuality preclude a mind for textuality?

Why must they be different?

In the streets, I'm a bigender person living with HIV, eager for attention and recognition.

In the sheets, I'm a bigender person living with HIV, eager for attention and recognition.

The Untold Story of Actaeon
(or, If Actaeon Was a Metaphor for HIV)

When Actaeon found love inside a lake,
That too pure love turned him from man to beast,
And in those misty woods, he ran with ache:
From shame he ran and ran, but shame increased.
When men spy him around the town, they warn
Any and all who love those beasts with fur:
"Keep far from him. Heed all, beware his horn.
Nor dare ye walk to lakes where curs'd men were."
The deer turns back; from hope he's shunned again.
He's still himself and still a man, but still
The curse is his; it cannot spread to men.
But they don't hear his tearing words nor will.
    He lets his hungry hounds rip out his heart
    And from this weary world his thoughts depart.

the walking dead

part of me
is still dead
still sitting
in a chair
at the clinic.
but now
i walk as the
undead.
a zombie
that just
does not
know
how to
die.
i'm still
around and
i'm still
looking
for someone
with a
brain.

Numbers and Letters

When I was first diagnosed,
a world of numbers
and letters
was thrown at me.

What is HIV? What is AIDS? What is the CDC? What is the
NIH? What is GRID? What is the 4-H disease? What is ADAP?
What is MIDAP? What is AZT? What is ART? What does U=U
mean? What is LAAN? What is CD4? What is an ID specialist?
What is EIS? What's my CD4 count? What's my viral load count?
How many pills do I have left? How many pills do I have to have
left before I can call in a refill? What number do I dial for refills?
What number do I dial if I have no refills left? What number do I
dial if I have questions? What's my doctor's number? How much
does my medication cost? How much does it cost with insurance?
What's the cost of therapy to deal with people telling me to kill
myself? How many vials of blood are you taking this time? How
many more months till my next appointment?

A hundred questions I didn't know the answer to
but I learned.

Chasing Cars

Last fall,
    I walked across campus,
        craving a vanilla latte
            laced with cinnamon.

The lawn was empty,
    not a student in sight,
        but the street at the edge
            of campus was busy.

I remember
    standing on the sidewalk
        and watching the cars
            pass me by.

The briefest
    thought crossed my mind:
        Jump, and it's all over.
        Just one jump.

It weighs on you,
    the number of people who
        tell you to make that jump
            when you've got

                      what I've got.

Are You in Good Hands?

After undergrad, I was uninsured.
I made about 1,000 dollars a month.
That was it.
Full-time grad student in America.
Lucky fucking me.

Then I got HIV.

Because I make so little, I get federal assistance
from having HIV.
The Ryan White program.
It saved my life.
In more ways than you know.

The cost to make a month's supply of HIV meds
Something like 100 dollars.
That's how much they cost in a lot of European countries.
Some places sell them for 20 dollars.

In America?

My pills for a month cost 5,000 dollars.

The first time I saw that
on the RiteAid pharmacy register display,
I wanted to kill myself.

If I can't afford it, might as well, right?
Or HIV would take me itself.

My Ryan White covers it. 100 percent.
But I'm terrified.
Will there be a day that that's cut?
Will there be a day that Repugnants say

"We don't want to pay for your bad decisions"
and axe the funding?
Will there be a day when I have to choose again?

Whether I let the HIV slowly kill me

or do it myself?

i think my mom's expecting me to die

when i first told her
she asked how much longer i had left

when i told her about my drugs
she told me there'd probably be side effects
fifty years from now that'll kill me
like cancer

when i was single
she said i should lower my standards
that no normal guy
would ever date
someone like me

when covid hit
she called and asked how it affects me
i told her it was the same as everybody else
she didn't believe me

i'm convinced
if i got hit by a car
she'd say it was hiv
or god's will
which, for her, might be the same.

neon

i'm a 28-year-old
gay person
craving
neon lights
and electric swing.

i sit at the bar
and order
pink drinks
from a ghost,
a bartender
who's not there
and hasn't been
for twenty years,

when an old man
sits beside me,
a pleather cap
a weathered harness
weathered skin
as transparent
as the genocide
the 80s allowed,

and says
i'm too young
to be in a place
like this.

i offer
a half-smile
and peel
open my shirt
where we keep
biohazard

symbols
branded
on our bare
chests.

he shakes his head
and says
i'm not allowed
to wear
that brand, "not
until you watch
your friends
and every lover
you've ever had
die
and watch their names
pile up
in the newspaper
like an index
or a grocery list
or ingredients,
so many
and all in black
and white.
you'll never know
what it was like
back then.
you've got it easy."

so i leave the club,
this neon cemetary,
the abandoned stripper pole
the sex swing with buckets of Crisco.
i walk through the rain
try to scrub away my Black Spot

and head to the club

for gays my age
where they dance all night
and all morning.

when they see the brand though
they stop
and stare
the strobe light shuts off
the DJ pauses Lady Gaga.

and all as one
they hold up their phones
and show me their screens

KILL YOURSELF
KILL YOURSELF
KILL YOURSELF
KILL YOURSELF
KILL YOURSELF
KILL YOURSELF
KILL YOURSELF

i retreat outside
back into the rain
and sit on the curb.

i clutch my chest,

for i'll never see
or hear
the neon ghosts
who sit
beside me.

our glow
is just
too quiet.

People Suck (or, if Allen Ginsberg wrote about AIDS)

In the past five years, I have witnessed a side of humanity I
never thought existed,
people who hate, judge, and ridicule you based on a blood test,
who send you a DM on Twitter at 2am to send you a meme of
      yourself as a stick figure portrayed as a slut who should
      have kept their legs closed, and then immediately apol-
      ogize because they forgot to add text and then send the
      revised version as if NOW it's ok
who read your sad erotica story for a FurPlanet anthology
      where one of the characters is struggling with HIV
      and then tell you, as a beta reader, that maybe you're
      being self-serving by talking about HIV, that maybe you
      should leave that kind of talk for people who don't have
      it, because they're the objective ones, and you're biased
who message you on Facebook because you lived in McTyeire
      Hall together years ago and ask you who pozzed you
      and ask what it was like and ask if you wanted it and ask
      how kinky it was and ask if you can poz them
and you still don't really know who he is but you remember
      seeing him across the dining room and you remember
      his name and you remember your friend Emily sitting
      there from time to time but you only knew him as the
      silent type who always sat at a different dinner table in
      the dorms
who, even if they are old and gay, look you in the eyes over the
      books at Barnes & Noble with a wrinkled smile and tell
      you with all the best intentions that you're overreacting,
      that it's not as bad as it used to be and you should quit
      worrying, that your worries and fears and anxieties are
      invalid now that there's medicine and then go back to
      their books
who block you on Grindr after you liked their profile and they
      respond with LOL I don't fuck with diseased people
while others tell you to kill yourself or ask if they can put you

down like you're a mongrel in the streets dying of parvo
and they think they're doing society and the dog a favor
by shooting it once or twice or—oops, still missing the
head LOL—three or four times
and others tell you OMG they're so sorry and want to know
everything about what happened because now that you
clicked that STAR by their name you owe them a full
medical report and life story so they can judge whether
you're a good-gay-with-HIV or a bad-gay-with-HIV
because how you got it determines whether they want to
ask what your name is or not
who look at you, not knowing your life, and say with every in-
tent to offend and without fear of being seen as wrong
You Should Have Worn a Condom
who change their mind even as they're standing there in a white
McDavid jockstrap and decide they don't want to "risk
it" and put their pants back on leaving you naked on the
couch
who fuck every guy in the Lansing Gay Men's Chorus but when
they see you on Scruff tell you that they don't want to
"risk it" with you
who fuck you good and hard and cum inside you and then when
you ask them to help you get off they say they don't
want to get AIDS from touching your dick and now the
erection's gone
who go to Tabu Sex Club to fuck and cum and see you, a hot,
skinny twink, and probe their rheumatic hands over
your smooth stomach and bulge in your AliExpress-or-
dered thong and you're completely naked while they're
completely clothed in the middle of the club and they
lean forward to your ear and you can hear them over the
bass of Lady Gaga and Ke$ha remixed a hundred times
over and you hear him ask are you clean and you don't
know how to answer
because you feel clean and you showered and you douched like a
good bottom and you take your meds and you get tested

regularly but you still have HIV and Michigan law just
changed to say you don't have to disclose your status if
you're taking your meds but you also don't want to fuck
with serophobic guys on principle so you say—
who listen to your story and then tell you about their gay un-
cle—it's always an uncle—who got it and died as if this
confession now makes you both brothers in spirit
who put on two Trojan condoms after they learn about your
status
who walk in and ask to see proof of your recent test results
from Sparrow Medical Labs confirming you're undetect-
able and you feel the pressure to comply
who walk up to you after your TED Talk at MSU and tell you
that your story was very emotional and they walk away,
clutching their purses as tight as their beliefs, and will
probably only think about the poor diseased kid they
heard today when they're talking at a dinner party later
that evening
who see your call for erotic horror stories in an upcoming
volume called Sinister Sheets and then submit stories of
people intentionally giving others HIV and then describ-
ing how they die, not realizing that it's not erotic that it's
not realistic and that the only horror is in the irony that
they don't realize the editor they sent it to has that virus
and lives the horror
who wear a badge on their left breast with the word KAREN
and have blonde hair and bleach-white skin and tell you
that it is irresponsible reckless unethical evil immoral for
you to have sex protected or not, that if they were you
they just wouldn't have sex again—just saying—
and you are stuck with the responsibility to make sense of the
noise, make sense of the din flooding your ears and eyes
and you can't cry out or you've failed and you can't bark
back too hard or they'll kill you and you can't bark too
much or you're self-serving
while you cower there shaking like a bitch in heat and other

hounds come and sniff and rim and fuck your hole
while you're still shaking and then they piss on you when
they're done and call you unclean and and call you slut
and say you deserved it and say that you're diseased
but you keep on trying to grin, your teeth showing, as you
educate the masses on what it's like to have HIV in 21st
century America.
All they see is a piss- and cum-covered mutt fooling itself into
thinking it's worth love, howling at

nothing.

Old, Sick Dog

No one buys the old dogs
No one buys the sick ones
They cost too much
They die too fast.
So I guess I'm an old, sick dog.
I spend so long looking for
love
that I sometimes just lie
against the bars
pretending they're just cold arms
hugging me tight.
I don't feel sick
But the price displayed on my cage
keeps dropping
And I'll always wonder—
always
—if my lover got me
because I'm cheap.
I'll always wonder
if he'll one day realize
he doesn't have to have
a sick dog.

Remus Lupin

The werewolf howls a nocturne
at the moon; the swollen disc's ascent
illuminates the wintry grove,
the beast's undulating fur, masking
the tears along his snout
and the flesh scarred from stones thrown
and bullets fire—silver. The blood
is hot, too, steaming like his breath
in the cold, and the tenor of his howl
sparks in the air like a mistake borne
of a bitch bred in heat.

The howl echoes throughout
the midnight wood; the town sleeps
through sound and fury, knowing they signify
nothing, and they will wake the next
day, telling tales of beasts and beauties,
but even the beasts in witches' rhymes
and the burning Birnam Wood, beasts
like me perhaps, have beauty inside,
with that midnight melody, singing
in their veins like water, like blood,
like a lover's warmth, like poison. The music
crescendos then fades, and when the song dies,
he walks back home, tail between his legs: tale
as old as time: who could ever love a beast?

The Symbols I Carry

A small plush black model of my virus
Cute and cuddly
Reminds me that it's not evil

My original test results
Stored in a cardboard box in my closet
Reminds me of my first pain

My phone case has an art piece
Of a furry version of me
Reading a book and holding a mug
With a big black ✚ on it

Reminds me to take some coffee
With my pain

A biohazard burning
In the back of my mind
The only symbol
I haven't got a physical form of,
Because I'm scared
Of what it'll remind me of.

January 7, 2015

once a year
Facebook reminds me
it shows me my most
popular
post from years ago
the one that got
38 comments
lots of
i'm sorry
and
you're strong
and
you can do this
i can't stop myself
i never can
i open the original post
and i read it
my desperation
my hopelessness
my fear
my suicidal ideation
and i can hear my wails
from the past
i feel that scared
21-year-old
still crying in my chest
i don't think
he ever stopped
i want to hold him
and tell him things will be
OK
and that he's not alone
and he'll still be loved

but i know the truth
even when i'm loved
i always worry
the other shoe is going to drop
and i'll be left alone
again
me and my HIV
i'm trying to heal
i'm trying so
fucking hard

i was lied to once
by someone i trusted
he had cheated on me
and made me feel special
and had a whole other life
and i was the one
in the dark
still am

every January
when I read that post
it all rushes back
the hurt
the betrayal
the fear
the shame
the loneliness

i don't know what to tell the past version of myself
i don't know how to comfort him
so i just read the post
and cry

why me?
i ask

to the emptiest room
no one has ever seen
why me?

The AIDS Monster

The most common question
I ever get is:
How did you get HIV?
Who gave it to you?

They envision a monster
some dark, hulking
silhouette
that walks around
pozzing every boy he sees.

They look for that person to blame.
To hate.

And the reality is
he was a dick.
He did lie to me.
He did know he had it.
He did tell me he was "clean."

But when you know all the shit
people like me have to put up with.
All the death threats
All the names.
I don't see him as that
dark, hulking
monster.

Just another person with HIV
trying to survive,
find love
in the only way he knew how.

When people—

people like my mom
or like the news reporter
or the guy on Grindr—
tell us that people with HIV
don't deserve to have
love,
some people are going to lie
about their status.

Was my ex an AIDS monster?
No. No more than I am.

He was just a guy
looking to be accepted.
And the way he sought that
got someone else hurt.

I don't blame him.
Even if he lied,
it takes two to tango.

Bag of Bugs

To the person who called me
a "bug bag" this morning
March 17, 2021,
because I didn't respond
to "hello"
within five minutes:

Here are the bugs
I've collected over the years.

In 2015, I was diagnosed
with HIV.

That same day, I learned
I also had chlamydia.

A year later, I got
my first case
of gonorrhea.

I've had both of those
a few times.

Once, I even had
Hepatitis B.

Got syphilis in 2019.
That shot sucked.

Well, I got my blood drawn
a month ago. Got my tests back.

Syphilis -
Hep B -

Gonorrhea -
Chlamydia -
HIV undetectable

I'm not crawling
with bugs.
But I'm no longer
afraid
when one lands on me.

When The Lion King's
Simba slurped up a
grub, he looked at
the camera—
at me—
and said,

slimy yet satisfying.

Impostor Syndrome

When people call me brave
for being open and vocal,
my instinct is to flinch.
How can they not realize
this is all an act?
How can they not see that
I call myself a slut as much
as they do, that I call myself
unclean as much as they do,
that past me wouldn't fuck
present me. How can they
not know that the only reason
I didn't kill myself was
because I'm actually
a coward?

Familiar

Sometimes I like to pretend
I have a pet demon.
He's a giant goat-man
with yellow eyes
and a biohazard symbol
emblazoned on his chest.
His wool is black as night,
and he exhales smoke
with each breath.

I didn't always have him.
I never wanted him.
But I got him.

He never says a word.
Just stands there
right over my shoulder.
Always within reach.

I was scared of him
for the longest time.
But I grew to love him
as a part of myself.

And when I sat on
the bathtub floor,
bawling and wishing
I had never been born,
he would put a hoof
on my shoulder
and just hold me.

Do you know what it's like
to feel so alone with your demons
that it feels like your demon's
the only one who really understands?

VIRAL

This poem is made up of exact quotes, things that have been
said to me after knowing I am HIV positive undetectable. These
lines are all from different people, but together they make the
din in my ears I've heard since January 7, 2015.

Why are you on here?
Why are you here?
You should have kept your legs closed.
You should have worn protection.
Did you learn your lesson?
It's what you get for being gay.
If I were you, I just wouldn't have sex anymore.
Just saying.
You're just going to infect everyone.

not into disease
sorry not into filthy sluts
not interested in getting disease
sorry
LOL
Why are you on here?

Is sharing straws safe?
Do I need to start wearing gloves now?
Oh Jonny, how much longer do you have?

At least it's not as bad as it was.
It's not as bad as it used to be.
Be thankful it's not like it was back in the 80s.
It's not a problem nowadays.
You need to quit being so self-serving with this.

If you don't mind my asking—
Hope you don't mind—

Is it alright if I ask—
How did you get it?
How did you get HIV?
Were you wanting to get it?
Why didn't you—
Who gave it to you?
Did he know he had it?
You didn't ask to see his papers?
Why not?

wait youre positive?
sorry i just now saw that
I'll wear two condoms, just in case!
ddf?
your poz? LOL no thanks

It's no big deal.

I wish people like you would just go kill yourselves.

HIV isn't poetic - reprise

nothing rhymes with HIV
there aren't too many metaphors
to compare it to even.

HIV, it's not like the snow
or the rain
or the wind
or a cold December night
or a busy morning in New York.

it's not something you read aloud
standing in front of a busy cafe
and expect people to nod their heads
as if they understand it all
as if they're taking something
meaningful from it.
they'll go back to their frappes
and their phones and forget all about this.
and when they go home,
they'll still message someone
on Grindr, asking,
"Hey, u clean?"

HIV isn't poetic.
It's personal, yeah.
It's political, sure.
But it can't be poetic.

If it was, wouldn't I walk away
from this with a greater knowledge
of the universe?
Or feel better about things?
Or about myself?

Or maybe I really don't know
that much about poetry.
Or about the universe.
Or even myself.

What if HIV was poetic?
What would it rhyme with?
What season would it most be like?
How many people would snap
their fingers all in chaotic unison
after the poem was said and done?
How much more of the world—
and myself—
would I suddenly understand?

Or maybe I'm asking all the wrong questions.

Maybe the poem is me, or some part of me,
or some version of my life story.
And maybe I am my HIV. Or it's a part of me,
or a part of me that's even deeper than just skin-deep.
And the HIV is me.

Not sure if that helps me solve the universe,
but you know…
I think it helps me live in it.
Just a little bit easier.
Just a bit.

Who knows what the future holds?
Things will get better.
They just have to.

I'm positive...